Healt

MW00917228

Dessert Recipes

No Sugar Added!

Ice Pops, Slushes, Sorbet, Treats on Sticks, Frozen Yogurt, Frozen drinks, Pies, Bars, Parfaits and More

Sarah Spencer

DISCLAIMER

Disclaimer and Terms of Use: Effort has been made to ensure that the information in this book is accurate and complete. However, the author and the publisher do not warrant the accuracy of the information, text, and graphics contained within the book due to the rapidly changing nature of science, research, known and unknown facts and internet. The Author and the publisher do not hold any responsibility for errors, omissions or contrary interpretation of the subject matter herein. This book is presented solely for motivational and informational purposes only.

The recipes provided in this report are for informational purposes only and are not intended to provide dietary advice. A medical practitioner should be consulted before making any changes in diet. Additionally, recipe cooking times may require adjustment depending on age and quality of appliances. Readers are strongly urged to take all precautions to ensure ingredients are fully cooked in order to avoid the dangers of foodborne viruses. The recipes and suggestions provided in this book are solely the opinion of the author. The author and publisher do not take any responsibility for any consequences that may result due to following the instructions provided in this book.

CONTENTS

INTRODUCTION

Once the warm weather hits, our taste buds seem to crave a different taste sensation. We desire freshness and sweetness that both satisfy and refresh. The only problem with traditional summer treats is that they tend to be a little too heavy on sugar and calories, while not fully utilizing the freshness of seasonal ingredients. When you decide to use what nature has to offer, you will find that there is less need for added sugars and artificial flavors. We have created this book to show you how to create tasty frozen summer treats that are sugar free and for the most part, guilt free as well. You can have the creaminess of ice cream, the leisurely pleasure of an ice pop and frozen drinks that are unparalleled in flavor.

This book has been specially created for those like you, who desire to live and eat with as little added sugar and sweeteners as possible. Eliminating refined sugars from your diet has many benefits, including controlling diabetes, managing weight control and reducing your risk of very serious health conditions such as cardiac disease. Everything that we put in our bodies should be meant to nourish and protect it. However, this does not mean that we cannot take pleasure in the foods that we eat, especially the frozen sweet treats of summer.

In some instances, ingredients such as honey or dark chocolate have been included as options to enhance the flavor of the dessert. Depending on your own personal health circumstances and dietary goals, it is up to your discretion if you wish to incorporate them into your recipe. Honey has been chosen because it is not refined like white sugar, it's natural, and just a little goes a long way in enhancing richness and flavor. When using chocolate, always choose a chocolate that has at least a 70% cocoa content. These chocolates are usually of the highest quality and lowest added sugar. Pay attention to the nutritional labels when choosing which chocolate to use. Although this was not included in any of the recipes, you may choose to add artificial, or alternative, sweeteners into the recipes to balance some of the tartness, especially with the fresh fruit recipes. It is suggested that if you choose an alternative sweetener that you use one that is as natural as possible, such as stevia.

I hope you enjoy the recipes in this book and take advantage of the many ways you can enjoy summer treats while reducing your sugar intake and keeping your health at the front of your priorities. Summertime is for sharing. Enjoy these recipes with friends and family and create new traditions and memories for years to come.

GRANITAS AND ICES

Simple and refreshing, granitas and ices instantly satisfy cold, sweet cravings on a hot summer day. Traditionally made with sugar or syrup, these recipes rely on the natural sweetness of fresh ingredients to bring the flavors to life.

Citrus Berry Granita

Summer time is the perfect opportunity to take advantage of the sweet, natural juiciness of ripe berries. This cooling granita combines berries with citrus to provide a refreshing, light treat on a hot day.

Serves: 4

Ingredients
1 cup fresh strawberries, quartered
1 cup fresh raspberries
½ cup fresh blueberries
½ cup fresh orange juice (no additional sugar added)
½ cup fresh grapefruit juice (no additional sugar added)
1 tablespoon fresh lime juice

Directions

1. Add the strawberries, raspberries, and blueberries to a blender or food processer and blend until smooth.
2. Using a fine mesh strainer, press the berry puree through to remove chunks and seeds.
3. Place the berry puree into a shallow baking dish and stir in the orange juice, grapefruit juice, and lime juice. Mix well.
4. Shake or smooth out the puree so that the surface is even and place the pan in the freezer.
5. After an hour remove the pan from the freezer and stir or scrape with a fork. Continue doing this once an hour until mixture is icy and slushy.
6. Serve in well-chilled glasses.

Grapefruit and Tonic Ice

Grapefruit and tonic has long been a favorite combination for summertime alcoholic beverages, traditionally served with gin. This version takes away the extra sugar and calories of the alcohol, but leaves all the refreshing tartness of grapefruit with just a hint of basil to balance it out.

Serves: 4

Ingredients

4 cups fresh grapefruit juice (no additional sugar added)

2 cups ice

1 cup sugar free tonic water

1 tablespoon fresh basil, finely chopped

Addition fresh basil for garnish

Directions

1. Place the grapefruit juice and ice in a blender. Crush quickly to break up the ice just a little.
2. Add the tonic water and basil. Continue to crush until a slushy, icy consistency forms. Add more ice if needed or desired.
3. Pour into well-chilled glasses and garnish with fresh basil to serve.

Espresso Granita with Coconut Cream

Sometimes you crave a frozen treat that is refreshing and invigorating, while not being overly fruity or sweet. This espresso granita does the trick. This can easily be made with decaffeinated espresso and served as an after dinner beverage or dessert.

Serves: 4

Ingredients

2 cups strongly brewed espresso

1 teaspoon vanilla extract

1 12 ounce can unsweetened full fat coconut milk

1 tablespoon shredded, unsweetened coconut

Directions

1. Begin by brewing and cooling the espresso.
2. Place the unopened can of coconut milk in the refrigerator. Chill for 2-4 hours.
3. Add the espresso and vanilla to a shallow baking pan and stir well. Place the pan in the freezer.
4. After one hour, remove the pan and stir or scrape with a fork. Return the pan to the freezer and repeat once an hour until an icy, slushy consistency forms.

5. When the granita is close to being done, remove the coconut milk from the refrigerator. Spoon out the thick coconut cream that has risen to the top, and place in a mixing bowl. Briefly beat on high speed to create a thick, fluffy coconut cream.

6. Serve the granita in well-chilled classes, topped with coconut cream and shredded coconut.

Chai Coconut Milk Ice

Deliciously fragrant with exotic spices, this Chai Ice takes a traditionally warm beverage and turns it into a luscious summertime treat.

Serves: 4

4 cups unsweetened vanilla coconut milk

4 black tea bags

1 teaspoon vanilla extract

1 teaspoon cinnamon

1 teaspoon ginger

½ teaspoon ground cloves

½ teaspoon cardamom

2 cups ice

Directions

1. In a medium saucepan, heat the coconut milk over medium heat.
2. Add the teabags, vanilla, cinnamon, ginger, cloves, and cardamom. Remove from heat and let steep for 30 minutes.
3. Pour into a bowl and place in the refrigerator until well chilled.
4. Remove from the refrigerator and stir.

5. Pour the mixture and the ice into a blender or food processor. Blend until creamy, adjusting the amount of ice as needed to create desired consistency.
6. Serve in well-chilled glasses.

Sour Apple Granita

Reminiscent of old-time sour apple ice pops, this granita adds a bit of sophisticated twist to a warm weather favorite.

Serves: 4

Ingredients

2 cups granny smith apples, peeled and chopped

1 cup fresh, no sugar added apple juice

2 tablespoons fresh lemon juice

1 teaspoon fresh ginger, grated

Directions

1. Place the apples and apple juice in a blender or food processor. Blend until mixture is smooth and liquid.
2. Transfer the apple mixture to a shallow baking dish. Add the lemon juice and fresh ginger. Mix well.
3. Place the pan in the freezer to chill.
4. Remove from the freezer after one hour. Stir or scrape with a fork and return to the freezer. Repeat this once every hour until mixture is slushy and icy.
5. Serve in well chilled glasses.

Mojito Icy Slush

Gaining enough popularity in recent years to be a contender against the traditional margarita, the mojito offers a unique freshness without being too sweet. This non-alcoholic version honors those traditional flavors. Honey has been included in this recipe to cut the tartness of the lime, however it is just as delicious without.

Serves: 4

Ingredients

1 cup water

1 cup fresh squeezed lime juice

2 teaspoons fresh lime juice

2 tablespoons honey (optional)

½ cup fresh mint leaves, chopped

2 cups ice

Lime slices for garnish

Fresh mint for garnish

Directions

1. Add all of the ingredients, including the mint leaves, to a blender or food processor, leaving out the honey if desired.

2. Pulse until all ingredients are blended and mint is well incorporated.
3. Add the ice to the blender, adjusting the amount as desired.
4. Blend until a slushy, icy consistency is formed.
5. Serve in well-chilled glasses garnished with lime and mint.

Triple Melon Sorbet

If you have an ice cream maker at home, this is the perfect opportunity to create a frozen dessert that is refreshing and healthy. The sweetness of these three melons blends perfectly, however you can use any type of melon that you like in this recipe.

Serves: 4-6

Ingredients

2 cups watermelon, cubed

1 cup casaba melon, cubed

1 cup honeydew melon, cubed

¼ cup fresh mint, chopped

2 cups sparkling water

¼ cup fresh lime juice

Directions

1. Add the watermelon, casaba melon, honeydew melon, and mint to a blender or food processor. Blend until smooth.
2. Add the sparkling water and lime juice. Blend again until smooth and liquid.
3. Place the mixture in the refrigerator to chill for one hour.

4. Transfer the mixture to an ice cream maker and proceed per manufacturer's instructions.
5. Chill for 2-3 hours before serving in ice cold dishes.
6. Garnish with mint, if desired.

Green Tea and Peach Snow Cones

Do you have memories from your youth of sweet, sticky, cold snow cones that came directly from the vendor at the local summer carnival or fair? This recipe will take you back in time, but with a bit of a more adult and healthier twist.

Serves: 4

Ingredients

5 cups shaved ice

1 cup fresh brewed iced green tea

1 cup sugar free peach juice or concentrate

1 tablespoon fresh squeezed lime juice

Fresh mint to garnish, if desired

Paper snow cone cups for serving

Directions

1. Place equal amounts of ice into 4-5 snow cone cups. Tap down slightly as you are filling to allow the ice to settle.
2. In a bowl or pitcher combine the green tea, peach juice, and lime juice. Mix well.

3. Carefully the mixture pour over the ice, going slowly to completely saturate without making the mixture more liquid than ice.

4. Garnish with fresh mint before serving, if desired.

Tart Lemon Sorbet

Who doesn't crave a tall, ice cold glass of lemonade during the summer? This recipe takes lemonade and turns it up several refreshing notches. There is honey included in this recipe to cut some of the tartness of the lemon, however you will find it to be just as refreshing and delicious without.

Serves: 4

Ingredients

2 cups sugar free sparkling lemon water

1 cup fresh squeezed lemon juice

1 tablespoon vanilla extract

2 teaspoons fresh lemon zest

1 teaspoon fresh grated ginger

1 tablespoon honey (optional)

Directions

1. Add all ingredients to a bowl, omitting the honey if desired. Mix well and place in the refrigerator to chill for at least one hour.
2. Once mixture is well chilled, transfer to an ice cream maker and proceed per manufacturer's instructions.

3. Chill the finished product for several hours before serving.

Mint Tangerine Slush

This is a tropical, icy drink with the refreshing taste of mint added as a subtle undertone. The flavor brings to mind splashing waves on a balmy tropical beach.

Serves: 4

Ingredients

2 cups sugar free sparkling tangerine or orange water

1 cup fresh tangerine juice or concentrate

1 tablespoon grapefruit juice

1 tablespoon lime juice

½ cup fresh mint, chopped

3 cups ice

Fresh lime slices for garnish

Directions

1. Place the sparkling water, tangerine juice, grapefruit juice, lime juice, and mint in a blender. Pulse lightly to mix and to further chop the mint into smaller pieces.
2. Add the ice to a blender and crush until a slushy, icy consistency has formed.
3. Pour into well-chilled glasses and garnish with fresh lime slices.

Tropical Slushie

It is entirely possible to recreate the experience of an island vacation in your own home. Tropical fruit flavors and a hint of coconut milk will get you as close to a tropical sunset as possible without leaving your own yard. For an extra touch, serve this slushie in hollowed-out pineapples or coconut shells.

Serves: 4-6

Ingredients

3 cups sparkling water

1 cup coconut milk

2 medium bananas

1 cup papaya, cubed

3 cups ice

1 cup fresh orange juice (no additional sugar added)

1 cup fresh pineapple juice (no additional sugar added)

Fresh pineapple for garnish

Directions

1. Add the sparkling water, coconut milk, bananas, and papaya to a blender and process until completely smooth.
2. Add the ice, orange juice, and pineapple juice. Blend until mixture reaches a slushy consistency.

3. Serve in well-chilled glasses garnished with pineapple.

FROZEN DRINKS

Warm weather calls for cool drinks. Each of these beverages offers refreshing flavors, with just enough sweetness to satisfy your summer sweet tooth. Most are incredibly easy to make and elegant enough to stand alone as a dessert.

Chocolate Raspberry Shake

Nothing beats the creaminess of a milk shake. Unfortunately, they are usually laden with calories and sugar. This version of a chocolate raspberry shake uses unsweetened almond milk combined with unexpected avocado to replace the creaminess that you would normally get from ice cream.

Serves: 4

Ingredients

2 cups unsweetened vanilla almond milk

1 cup frozen raspberries

1 avocado, peeled and cubed

1 ½ tablespoons dark cocoa powder

1 teaspoon vanilla extract

2 cups ice

Fresh raspberries for garnish

Chocolate shavings made from 70% or higher cocoa chocolate

Directions

1. Place the vanilla almond milk, raspberries, and avocado in a blender and blend until smooth.
2. Add the dark cocoa powder, vanilla extract, and ice. Blend until ice is crushed and the drink is thick, smooth, and creamy. Adjust the amount of ice if necessary to achieve the desired consistency.
3. Pour into frosty glasses and garnish with fresh raspberries and chocolate shavings, if desired.

Orange Cream Pop Float

Orange cream pop is a classic flavor. This float combines the convenience of packaged ice cream with the freshness of homemade sorbet. Finishing off with naturally flavored sparkling water, instead of sticky sweet soda, makes this the perfect summer treat.

Serves: 4

Ingredients

1 cups sugar free orange juice

1 cup peaches, peeled and cubed

1 tablespoon vanilla extract

1 cup unsweetened coconut milk

2 cups sugar free vanilla ice cream or sugar free rice ice milk

2 cups naturally flavored orange sparkling water

Directions

1. In a blender, combine the orange juice, peaches, vanilla extract, and coconut milk. Blend until creamy.
2. Pour the mixture into a shallow baking pan and place in the freezer.

3. After one hour, remove the pan and stir or scrape with a fork before returning to the freezer. Repeat this once an hour until a creamy, slushy consistency is formed.
4. In four well-chilled desserts cups alternate scoops of the orange cream sorbet and sugar free vanilla ice cream.
5. Top with the orange sparkling water before serving.

Frozen Hot Chocolate

No matter the weather, there is always a place for chocolate. This version of "hot chocolate" is cooling and creamy. Dark chocolate is used to minimize the amount of sugar, since high percentage, quality chocolate is generally very low. You may substitute with completely sugar free versions if you desire.

Serves: 4

Ingredients

½ cup 70% or higher dark chocolate pieces (you can substitute sugar free chocolate)

1 teaspoon dark cocoa powder

1 tablespoon vanilla extract

1 teaspoon cinnamon

4 cups unsweetened coconut milk

2 cups ice

Sugar free whipped topping, if desired

Directions

1. In a double boiler or microwave, gently melt the chocolate pieces.

2. In a saucepan, combine the dark cocoa powder, vanilla extract, cinnamon and coconut milk. Heat

over medium until mixture begins to bubble gently.

3. Slowly stir in the melted chocolate and continue to heat for 2 minutes.

4. Remove from heat, let cool slightly, and transfer to a bowl.

5. Chill in the refrigerator for at least 1 hour.

6. Combine the chocolate mixture with the ice in a blender. Blend until mixture is smooth and creamy.

7. Pour the thick mixture into four well-chilled glasses and top with sugar free whipped topping, if desired.

Banana Coladas

Sweet bananas and fresh pineapple replace the sugar in this taste of tropical paradise.

Serves: 4

Ingredients

2 medium bananas

1 cup fresh pineapple chunks

1 cup unsweetened coconut milk

½ cup naturally flavored lime sparkling water

1 cup ice

Lime slices to garnish

Directions

1. Combine the bananas, pineapple chunks, and coconut milk in a blender. Blend until creamy.
2. Add the sparkling water and ice. Blend until mixture is creamy and slushy.
3. Pour mixture into frosty glasses and garnish with fresh lime before serving.

Spicy Coffee Frozen Sipper

Not as heavy or complicated as most coffee flavored frozen treats, this drink is a quick, easy way to recharge on a summer day.

Serves: 2-4

Ingredients

4 cups brewed coffee

1 cup unsweetened coconut milk

2 teaspoons dark cocoa powder

1 teaspoon cinnamon

½ teaspoon cardamom

2 cups ice

Sugar free whipped topping, if desired

Directions

1. Add the brewed coffee, coconut milk, cocoa powder, cinnamon and cardamom to a blender. Blend until all ingredients are incorporated.
2. Add the ice cubes and blend until ice is crushed and drink is slushy.
3. Pour into chilled glasses and top with sugar free whipped topping, if desired.

Cinnamon and Coconut Milkshakes

The clean and classic flavor of a coconut milk shake is lightly spiced with a hint of cinnamon in this creamy, warm weather cooler.

Serves: 4

Ingredients

2 cups unsweetened vanilla coconut milk

½ cup unsweetened, shredded coconut

2 cups sugar free vanilla ice cream or sugar free frozen rice milk

2 teaspoons ground cinnamon

Cinnamon sticks for garnish

Sugar free whipped topping, if desired

Directions

1. Place all ingredients, except for the whipped topping, in a blender.
2. Blend in short bursts until the consistency is thick and creamy, but not too liquid.
3. Pour into chilled glasses and top with sugar free whipped topping and a cinnamon stick, if desired.

Frozen Cherry Lemonade

This frozen cherry lemonade is so much tastier and healthier than premade frozen slushies. With a dash of tartness and a bit of sweetness, this could become your favorite summer drink.

Serves: 2-4

Ingredients

3 cups fresh or frozen cherries, pits removed

1 tablespoon sugar free powdered lemonade mix

2 cups naturally flavored lemon sparkling water

1 tablespoon fresh lime juice

2 teaspoons fresh lime zest

2 cups ice

Lemon wedges for garnish

Directions

1. Place the cherries in a blender and set aside.
2. Mix the powdered lemonade mix with the sparkling water. Stir to dissolve completely.
3. Add the lemon sparkling water, lime juice, and lime zest to the blender. Mix briefly to incorporate the ingredients together.

4. Add the ice and blend until slushy in texture.

5. Transfer to well-chilled glasses and garnish with fresh lemon.

TREATS ON A STICK

Most home freezers stock an inventory of ice pops during the summer. Rather than purchasing them, take the opportunity to create these new flavors using fresh and healthy ingredients for your family.

Berry Melon Pops

If there is a quintessential taste of summer, it has to be watermelon. The sweet, juicy fruit is paired with blackberries and frozen into healthy ice pops.

Serves: 4-6

Ingredients

3 cups seedless watermelon, cubed

1 cup fresh blackberries

1 cup sparkling water

1 tablespoon fresh mint

Directions

1. Place the watermelon, blackberries, sparkling water, and fresh mint in a blender.
2. Blend until pureed and smooth.

3. Transfer the puree to ice pop molds and place in the freezer.

4. Freeze for at least 4 hours or overnight for best results.

Frozen Vanilla Banana Swirl Bars

If you enjoy frozen bananas you will love this treat. Rich and creamy, with the vanilla highlighting the fresh banana flavor, this is sure to be a favorite in your home.

Serves: 4

Ingredients

2 medium bananas

½ cup unsweetened coconut milk

½ teaspoon cinnamon

1 teaspoon honey (optional)

½ cup sugar free vanilla Greek yogurt

1 teaspoon vanilla extract

Directions

1. In a blender, combine the bananas, coconut milk, cinnamon, and honey, if using. Blend until smooth and transfer the mixture to a bowl.
2. Mix together the yogurt and vanilla extract before adding the yogurt to the banana mixture.
3. Stir just enough to swirl the yogurt into the banana mixture without completely mixing it in.

4. Spoon the mixture into ice pop molds and place in the freezer.

5. Freeze for at least 4 hours, or overnight for best results.

Mango Jigglers

Gelatin pops are a summertime staple in many children's lives. Here we elevate them to a frozen treat that adults will find irresistible as well.

Serves: 4-6

Ingredients

1 3 oz box sugar free orange flavored gelatin

1 cup boiling water

1 cup cold sparkling water

1 cup fresh mango, cubed

2 teaspoons fresh grated ginger

Directions

1. In a bowl combine the orange gelatin and boiling water. Stir to dissolve.
2. Add the cold sparkling water and set aside to cool.
3. In a blender combine the mango and grated ginger. Blend to desired consistency, either pureeing for a smooth ice pop or leaving the mango slightly chunky for larger bites of fruit in the finished product.
4. Add the gelatin mixture to the blender and pulse quickly once or twice to blend.

5. Transfer to ice pop molds and place in the freezer.
6. Freeze for at least 4 hours, or overnight for best results.

Mexican Choco Fudge Pops

This is a slightly spicy, but healthy take on the traditional chocolate fudge pop we all love. A few chocolate chips have been included, but are completely optional. If you choose to use them, use either sugar free or chips with a very high percentage of cocoa, which are generally very low in added sugar.

Serves: 4

Ingredients

1 cup sugar free vanilla Greek yogurt

1 cup unsweetened almond milk

1 tablespoon dark cocoa powder

1 teaspoon vanilla extract

2 teaspoons cinnamon

2 tablespoons extra dark or sugar free chocolate chips (optional)

Directions

1. In a blender combine the vanilla Greek yogurt, almond milk, cocoa powder, vanilla extract and cinnamon. Blend until creamy.

2. Spoon a few chocolate chips (optional) into each of the ice pop molds before topping with the chocolate mixture.

3. Place in the freezer and freeze for 4 hours, or overnight for best results.

Strawberries and Cream Bars

This recipe brings to mind the fresh strawberries and cream that tops decadent strawberry shortcake. The difference is that this recipe is easier, sugar free and less of a strain on the waistline.

Serves: 4

Ingredients

2 cups fresh strawberries, quartered

1 cup sugar free vanilla yogurt

½ cup unsweetened coconut milk

1 teaspoon vanilla extract

Directions

1. Combine the strawberries, vanilla yogurt, coconut milk and vanilla extract in a blender. Blend until desired consistency is reached, leaving a few chunks of strawberries, if desired.
2. Pour the mixture into ice pop molds and freeze for at least 4 hours, or overnight for best results.

Fruit Salad Pops

Do you love fruit salad? If so, it is time to take it out of the bowl and recreate it into a surprising frozen treat. Feel free to substitute your favorite fruits for the ones listed.

Serves: 4-6

Ingredients

½ cup mango, cubed

1 kiwi fruit, peeled and sliced

½ cup fresh raspberries

½ cup fresh peaches, peeled and cubed

1 cup naturally flavored lemon sparkling water

1 tablespoon lime juice

1 teaspoon lime zest

Directions

1. Carefully arrange the prepared fruit into the ice pops molds. The amount of fruit used will depend upon personal preference. Pack more fruit into the mold for a chunkier texture, and a little less for something more traditional.

2. Combine the lemon sparkling water, lime juice and lime zest.

3. Add the sparkling water mixture to each mold, tapping gently to make sure the liquid completely surrounds the fruit.
4. Place in the freezer and freeze for at least 4 hours, or overnight for best results.

Root Beer Float Pops

A bit of twist on the popular soda fountain treat, this ice pop layers a vanilla cream with rich, creamy root beer.

Serves: 4

Ingredients

2 cups sugar free root beer soda

½ cup heavy cream

1 can unsweetened coconut milk

1 teaspoon vanilla extract

Directions

1. A day before you plan to make the pops, place the can of coconut milk in the refrigerator.

2. When you're ready to begin, remove the coconut milk from the refrigerator and scoop out the solid layer of coconut cream that has collected at the top. Spoon into a bowl and combine with the vanilla extract. Spoon equal amounts into the tops of the ice pop molds.

3. Combine the root beer and heavy cream, stir gently while allowing some of the soda carbonation to settle down before adding to the molds.

4. Place in the refrigerator and freeze for at least 4 hours, or overnight for best results.

Italian Pistachio Pops

Not only is the flavor of pistachios a completely unexpected surprise, but the hint of cardamom and orange bring this frozen treat to the brink of exotic.

Serves: 4

Ingredients

½ cup sugar free vanilla Greek yogurt

½ cup heavy cream

2 tablespoons sugar free pistachio pudding mix

½ teaspoon orange extract

½ teaspoon cardamom

¼ cup crushed pistachios

Directions

1. In a blender, combine the yogurt, heavy cream, pudding mix, orange extract, and cardamom. Blend until smooth and creamy.
2. Pour the mixture into the ice pop molds.
3. Sprinkle a generous portion of crushed pistachios into each mold before placing in the freezer.
4. Freeze for at least 4 hours, or overnight for best results.

Creamy Mint Bars

The secret ingredient in this bar is avocado. Not only does the avocado add creaminess and contribute to the color, but it also accentuates the flavor of mint.

Serves: 4

Ingredients

1 cup sugar free vanilla yogurt

1 cup coconut milk

¼ cup avocado, cubed

¼ cup fresh mint leaves

2 teaspoons mint extract

Directions

1. In a blender combine the vanilla yogurt, coconut milk and avocado. Blend until creamy.
2. Add the mint leaves and mint extract. Blend until mint is finely chopped.
3. Pour the mixture into ice pop molds and place in the freezer.
4. Freeze for at least 4 hours, or overnight for best results.

Cucumber Lime Pops

If you are looking for a frozen summer treat that is more refreshing than it is sweet, than this is the one for you. Cucumbers take on an entirely different personality in this refreshing ice pop.

Serves: 4

Ingredients

1 cup cucumber, peeled and cubed

¼ cup fresh lime juice

1 tablespoon honey (optional)

1 tablespoon fresh mint, chopped

2 teaspoons fresh lime zest

1 cup naturally flavored lime sparkling water

Directions

1. Place the cucumber, lime, and honey, if using, in a blender. Blend until cucumber becomes liquefied.
2. Add the mint, lime zest, and sparkling water. Blend until well mixed.
3. Pour into ice pop molds and place in the freezer.
4. Freeze for at least 4 hours, or overnight for best results.

French Vanilla Cream Pop

Absolutely one of the simplest recipes for a classic flavored treat. This is pure simplicity at its finest.

Serves: 4

Ingredients

2 cups unsweetened coconut milk

1 cup sugar free vanilla yogurt

2 tablespoon sugar free vanilla pudding mix

1 vanilla bean, insides only

Directions

1. Place all of the ingredients in a blender and blend until creamy.
2. Transfer the mixture to the ice pop molds and place in the freezer.
3. Freeze for at least 4 hours or overnight for best results.

Sweet Surprises Banana Pops

These ice pop are especially fun for kids due to the sweet surprises tucked in the middle. Be creative and discover what unique flavors you can hide in the center of a banana pop.

Serves: 4-6

Ingredients

2 medium bananas

1 cup heavy cream or whole milk

1 teaspoon vanilla extract

½ teaspoon ground cinnamon

½ cup fresh strawberries, cut into small pieces

½ cup sugar free chocolate chips (optional)

Directions

1. Add the bananas, heavy cream, vanilla extract, and cinnamon to a blender. Blend until bananas are completely pureed.
2. Pour the mixture into the ice pop molds, filling only ¾ of the way.
3. Press the strawberries pieces and chocolate chips (optional) into the center of the pops.
4. Place in the freezer and freeze for at least 4 hours, or overnight for best results.

FROZEN YOGURTS

Frozen yogurt is a lighter, tangier and heather alternative to ice cream. Here we have highlighted some of the most amazing flavors and preparations of this creamy treat. The recipes included use an ice cream maker as part of the final process. If you do not have an ice cream maker, you can still create these delicious recipes. Simply prepare the yogurt the same you would for a granita. Mix the ingredients and place them in a shallow pan in the freezer. Every hour scrape or stir the mixture until it becomes frozen and slushy. While the texture may not be as creamy as with an ice cream maker, the flavor and freshness will shine through regardless of the preparation.

Apricot and Coconut Frozen Yogurt

Sweet apricot blends with tropical, creamy coconut in this lightly flavored frozen yogurt.

Serves: 4-6

Ingredients

2 cups full fat plain yogurt, preferably Greek

2 cups sugar free vanilla yogurt

½ cup unsweetened coconut milk

1 ½ cups apricots, cubed

½ cup unsweetened shredded coconut

Directions

1. Add the yogurts and coconut milk to a blender. Blend to liquefy the yogurt slightly.

2. Add the apricots and shredded coconut. Blend until smooth.

3. Place in the refrigerator and chill for at least one hour.

4. Add to your ice cream maker and proceed per manufacturer's instructions.

5. Once the process is complete, chill for at least one hour before serving.

Lime Basil Frozen Yogurt

Offering an incredible spin on lime sherbet, this garden fresh dessert is a surprising treat to the palette and makes for the perfect end to a summer dinner.

Serves 4-6

Ingredients

2 cups full fat plain yogurt, preferably Greek

2 cups sugar free vanilla yogurt

½ cup fresh lime juice

1 teaspoon vanilla extract

2 teaspoons honey (optional)

1 tablespoon lime zest

½ cup fresh basil

Directions

1. Combine all ingredients, excluding the honey if not using, in a blender. Blend until mixture is smooth and basil is finely chopped and incorporated throughout.
2. Place in the refrigerator and chill for at least one hour.
3. Add to your ice cream maker and proceed per manufacturer's instructions.

4. Once the process is complete, chill for at least one hour before serving.

Peanut Butter Frozen Yogurt

A treat that adults and children will both enjoy equally. If you are feeling adventurous, try adding fruit, such as berries, to this yogurt to create a peanut butter and jelly version.

Serves: 4-6

Ingredients

2 cups full fat plain yogurt, preferably Greek

2 cups sugar free vanilla yogurt

1 cup no sugar added creamy peanut butter

1 teaspoon walnut extract

½ cup chopped peanuts

Directions

1. Add the yogurts, peanut butter, and walnut extract to a blender. Blend until creamy.
2. Stir in the peanuts.
3. Place in the refrigerator and chill for at least one hour.
4. Add to your ice cream maker and proceed per manufacturer's instructions.
5. Once the process is complete, chill for at least one hour before serving.

Mexican "Fried" Frozen Yogurt

While not the caramel coated ball of ice cream you might associate with this dessert, this version highlights the flavor of cinnamon and vanilla with just a hint of honey.

Serves: 4-6

Ingredients

2 cups full fat plain yogurt, preferably Greek

2 cups sugar free vanilla yogurt

½ cup unsweetened coconut milk

1 cup unsweetened shredded coconut

2 teaspoons cinnamon

1 teaspoon vanilla extract

½ cup thin, crushed tortilla chips

1 tablespoon honey (optional)

Directions

1. Combine the yogurts, coconut milk, shredded coconut, cinnamon, and vanilla extract in a blender. Blend until creamy.
2. Stir in the crushed tortilla chips and honey, is using.
3. Place in the refrigerator and chill for at least one hour.

4. Add to your ice cream maker and proceed per manufacturer's instructions.

5. Once the process is complete, chill for at least one hour before serving.

Butterscotch Frozen Yogurt Buttons

These little butterscotch nuggets are the perfect tiny nibble on a warm day. Also a favorite with children, these finger food treats will disappear fast.

Serves: 6

Ingredients

2 cups full fat plain yogurt, preferably Greek

2 cups sugar free vanilla yogurt

½ cup sugar free vanilla almond milk

3 tablespoons sugar free butterscotch pudding mix

1 teaspoon cinnamon

Directions

1. Line a baking sheet with parchment paper.
2. Combine all of the ingredients in a blender and blend until completely smooth.
3. Using a pastry bag, make coin sized droplets of the yogurt mixture onto the parchment line baking sheet.
4. Place in the freezer for at least 4 hours, or overnight for best results.

Frozen Yogurt Fruit Bark

You may think of fruit bark as a wintertime holiday treat, however this recipe will make you rethink the stereotype. Creamy yogurt blended with fresh and dried fruit adds texture and depth to this dish.

Serves: 6

Ingredients

2 cups full fat plain yogurt, preferably Greek

2 cups sugar free vanilla yogurt

½ cup dried cranberries

½ cup unsweetened shredded coconut

1 tablespoon fresh orange zest

1 cup fresh blueberries

½ cup walnuts, chopped

½ cup sugar free chocolate chips (optional)

Directions

1. Line a 9x11" inch baking pan with parchment paper.
2. In a bowl, combine the yogurts with the cranberries, shredded coconut, and orange zest. Mix well.
3. Spread the yogurt mixture onto the parchment-lined pan.

4. Top with the blueberries, walnuts, and chocolate chips, if using.
5. Place in the freezer and freeze overnight.
6. Either cut into pieces or break apart by removing from the paper and breaking against the counter.
7. Store any uneaten pieces in a freezer bag in the freezer.

Mini Mocha Yogurt Tarts

These elegant and bite-sized mocha tarts are perfect for any occasion, from a special luncheon to a quick afternoon pick-me-up.

Serves: 6-8

Ingredients

2 cups full fat plain yogurt, preferably Greek

2 cups sugar free vanilla yogurt

1 cup strong brewed espresso

1 tablespoon dark cocoa powder

1 teaspoon vanilla extract

1 teaspoon rum extract

Sugar free chocolate chips for garnish, optional

Mini cupcake paper baking cups

Directions

1. Line a baking sheet with 15-18 mini baking cups.
2. In a blender combine the yogurts, brewed espresso, cocoa powder, vanilla extract and rum extract. Blend until smooth.
3. Spoon equal amounts of the mixture into mini baking cups.
4. Top with a sugar free chocolate chips, if desired.

5. Place in the freezer and freeze for at least 4 hours, or overnight for best results.

Strawberry Cheesecake Swirl Frozen Yogurt

Get all the richness and creaminess of strawberry cheesecake in a lower fat, sugar free frozen version with this frozen yogurt.

Serves: 4-6

Ingredients

2 cups full fat plain yogurt, preferably Greek

2 cups sugar free vanilla yogurt

½ cup cream cheese

2 teaspoons vanilla extract

1 ½ cups fresh strawberries, quartered

½ cup crushed sugar free vanilla wafers or graham crackers

1 teaspoon cinnamon

Directions

1. Combine the yogurts with the cream cheese and vanilla extract. Blend until creamy.
2. Add the strawberries, vanilla wafers or graham crackers, and cinnamon. Blend quickly just to slightly break apart the strawberries, still leaving a good amount of chunks.

3. Place in the refrigerator and chill for at least one hour.

4. Add to your ice cream maker and proceed per manufacturer's instructions.

5. Once the process is complete, chill for at least one hour before serving.

Frozen Yogurt Covered Strawberries

More refreshing than traditional chocolate-covered strawberries, these elegant strawberries have the perfect amount of sweetness and are cool for an easy summer treat.

Serves: 6-8

Ingredients

24 whole large fresh strawberries

1 ½ cup sugar free vanilla Greek yogurt

1 teaspoon orange extract

½ cup crushed pretzel pieces

Directions

1. Begin by washing the strawberries and lining a baking sheet with parchment paper.
2. Place the whole strawberries in the freezer for one hour to thoroughly chill.
3. Combine the Greek yogurt and orange extract in a bowl.
4. Dip each strawberry in the yogurt and immediately dip the tip in crushed pretzels.
5. Place back on the baking sheet and return to the freezer.

6. Freeze for at least 4 hours, or overnight for best results.

Pumpkin Spice Creamy Treat

Pumpkin spice does not have to be reserved for the fall. You can enjoy every bit of the spicy, rich goodness during the dog days of summer as well.

Ingredients

2 cups full fat plain yogurt, preferably Greek

2 cups sugar free vanilla yogurt

½ cup canned pumpkin puree (no additional sugar added)

1 teaspoon cinnamon

1 teaspoon nutmeg

1 teaspoon ginger

Directions

1. Combine all of the ingredients in a blender and blend until smooth and creamy.
2. Place in the refrigerator and chill for at least one hour.
3. Add to your ice cream maker and proceed per manufacturer's instructions.
4. Once the process is complete, chill for at least one hour before serving.

PIES, BARS AND OTHER TREATS

These desserts are a little unconventional—they're the ones to surprise your friends and family with! From frozen pies to unexpected frozen cookie bars, you are sure to find both personal favorites and crowd pleasers here.

Frozen Banana Split Pie

All of the flavors of a banana split mingle together in this frozen warm weather pie.

Serves: 8

Ingredients

2 medium bananas

1 cup sugar free vanilla yogurt

1 cup sugar free vanilla wafers or graham crackers

1 cup fresh strawberries, quartered

½ cup cream cheese

1 cup fresh pineapple, cut into small tidbits

½ cup sugar free chocolate chips

2 cups sugar free whipped topping

Directions

1. In a blender, combine the bananas, vanilla yogurt, and vanilla wafers or graham crackers. Blend until creamy, and spread in the bottom of an 8 inch pie dish.
2. Add the strawberries and cream cheese to the blender and blend until creamy. Layer this mixture over the banana mixture.
3. Top with fresh pineapple chunks and sugar free chocolate chips.
4. Place in the freezer, and freeze overnight.
5. Top with whipped topping before serving.

Frozen Five Layer Heaven Bars

This multi-layered bar provides a sweet taste of heaven. Avoid the heat of the oven by turning to this version of a popular cookie bar.

Serves: 10-12

Ingredients

1 cup sugar free vanilla Greek yogurt

1 cup cream cheese

1 tablespoon vanilla extract

1 cup cashews, chopped

½ cup strawberries, chopped

1 tablespoon sugar free strawberry gelatin

½ cup boiling water

5-6 ice cubes

1 cup shredded unsweetened coconut

1 cup sugar free chocolate chips, or extremely high cocoa percentage chocolate chips

Directions

1. Line a 9x9" baking pan with parchment paper.
2. In a blender combine the vanilla yogurt, cream cheese and vanilla extract. Spread the mixture in the bottom of the parchment lined pan.

3. Top the cream cheese mixture with chopped cashews.

4. Combine the sugar free strawberry gelatin with the boiling water and stir to dissolve. Add the fresh strawberries and crush to break apart just slightly. Add a few ice cubes to expedite the chilling process. Pour the mixture over the pan.

5. Top with a generous layer of shredded coconut and chocolate chips.

6. Place in the freezer and freeze overnight.

7. Cut into twelve squares before serving.

Coconut Almond Creamy Frozen Parfaits

This multilayered creamy parfait takes advantage of lower calorie and sugar free ingredients to recreate the sugary, cold dense sundae parfait.

Serves: 4

Ingredients

2 cans unsweetened coconut milk

1 cup sugar free whipped topping

1 cup fresh cherries, pits removed

1 tablespoon orange juice

1 teaspoon vanilla extract

1 cup almonds, sliced

½ cup sugar free vanilla wafers or graham crackers, crushed

½ cup unsweetened shredded coconut

Additional fresh cherries and whipped topping for garnish, if desired.

Directions

1. The day before preparing, place the cans of coconut milk in the refrigerator and let chill overnight.

2. The next day, remove the cans from the refrigerator and scoop out the thick coconut cream that has risen to the top. Place this in a medium sized bowl.

3. Add the sugar free whipped topping to the bowl and mix on low speed until creamy and fluffy. Place the bowl in the freezer to chill briefly.

4. Meanwhile add the cherries, orange juice and vanilla extract to a small sauce pan. Heat over medium heat until cherries begin to break down slightly, approximately 7 minutes.

5. Remove from heat and let cool completely.

6. In a small bowl combine the vanilla wafers or graham crackers with the shredded coconut.

7. Once cherries have cooled, begin to layer ingredients in dessert glasses. Start with a bit of the coconut cream in the bottom of each glass, followed by a layer of sliced almonds, cherries and cookie coconut mixture. Repeat until all ingredients have been used.

8. Place in the freezer to chill for 1-2 hours.

9. Top with a dollop of whipped topping and fresh cherry if desired.

Chocolate Peanut Butter Madness Frozen Mousse

Pure cocoa butter adds a rich, extremely creamy texture to this frozen mousse. The nutty, slightly butter flavor perfectly complements the peanut butter in this dish.

Serves: 4

Ingredients

1 can unsweetened coconut milk

1 cup food grade cocoa butter, cut into small pieces

½ cup no sugar added creamy peanut butter

1 tablespoon dark cocoa powder

1 teaspoon vanilla extract

¼ peanuts, chopped

Directions

1. The day before, place the can of coconut milk in the refrigerator and allow to chill overnight.

2. Remove the thick coconut cream that has risen to the top of the can and place in a saucepan. Add the peanut butter, cocoa powder and vanilla extract. Heat over medium heat until creamy and bubbly.

3. Put the cocoa butter into a bowl and pour the peanut butter mixture over the top of it.

4. Stir until creamy and cocoa butter is completely melted.
5. Pour into serving glasses and place in the freezer for at least 4 hours.
6. Garnish with chopped peanuts before serving.

Chocolate Avocado and Almond Freezer Pudding

This dessert is creamy and elegant enough to serve at a dinner party, and your guest will never suspect that the rich creaminess comes from cool avocado.

Serves: 4-6

Ingredients

2 cups prepared sugar free chocolate pudding1 cup avocado, cubed

1 teaspoon vanilla extract

1 teaspoon almond extract

1 cup sugar free whipped topping

½ cup sliced almonds

Directions

1. In a blender, combine the prepared chocolate pudding with the avocado, vanilla extract and almond extract. Blend until creamy and the avocado is well mixed in. Transfer to a bowl.

2. Gently fold in the sugar free whipped topping. Stir gently until the whipped topping is just mixed in.

3. Transfer to serving dishes and place in the freezer for at least 4 hours.

4. Top with sliced almonds before serving.

Chili Mango Freezer Bars

A little bit of spice and a whole bunch of cool are the perfect compliments for a summer dessert. For an extra touch, serve these freezer bars with fresh tropical fruit.

Serves: 8-12

Ingredients

2 cups sugar free vanilla Greek yogurt

½ cup cream cheese

1 tablespoon fresh lemon juice

2 tablespoons sugar free orange gelatin powder

1 cup boiling water

½ cup chopped ice

1 cup fresh mango, cubed

½ teaspoon cayenne pepper powder

½ cup pistachios, ground

Directions

1. Line a 9x9" baking pan with parchment paper.
2. In a blender combine the vanilla yogurt, cottage cheese and lemon juice. Blend until creamy. Spread this mixture into the bottom of the lined baking pan.

3. In a bowl combine the orange gelatin powder with the boiling water. Stir to dissolve. Add the chopped ice to shorten the cooling time.

4. Meanwhile, add the mango and cayenne powder to a blender and puree until smooth. Add the gelatin mixture in and pulse quickly to mix.

5. Pour the mango mixture over the cream mixture in the pan. Spread evenly.

6. Top with ground pistachios.

7. Place in the freezer and freeze for at least 4 hours, or overnight for best results.

8. Cut into 12 squares before serving.

Frozen Lemon Poppyseed Truffles

These truffles are easier to make than traditional truffles and filled with every bit of deliciousness. Fresh lemon and poppyseed highlight summers flavor, while a bit of lavender adds an unexpected touch.

Serves: 8

Ingredients

1 cup sugar free vanilla yogurt

2 tablespoons poppy seeds

1 tablespoon fresh lemon juice

2 teaspoons fresh lemon zest

1 teaspoon fresh lavender, ground

¼ cup coconut oil, melted

¼ cup coconut flour

1 cup pistachios, ground

Directions

1. In a bowl combine the vanilla yogurt, poppy seeds, lemon juice, lemon zest, and lavender. Mix Well.

2. To the bowl add the melted coconut and coconut flour. Mix well to combine. Mixture should be thick, but too wet to form. Adjust the amount of coconut flour as needed.

3. Place the bowl in the refrigerator and let set for 15-20 minutes.
4. Line a baking sheet with parchment paper.
5. Remove the bowl and quickly form bite size balls from the mixture using your hands. The heat from your hands will cause the mixture to begin to soften. You may need to place the mixture back in the refrigerator if it becomes too soft.
6. Roll each ball in the ground pistachios and place on the baking sheet.
7. Place the truffles in the freezer for at least 4 hours, or overnight for best results.

Frozen Cream Cheese Fudge Bites

These little bites take the best of traditional fudge pops and rich fudge candies and blend together to create the perfect rich chocolate bite size treat.

Serves: 6-8

Ingredients

1 cup cream cheese

½ cup sugar free vanilla Greek yogurt

1 tablespoon dark cocoa powder

1 tablespoon vanilla extract

2 teaspoons honey (optional)

1 tablespoon strong brewed coffee

Chocolate covered espresso beans for garnish (optional)

Directions

1. Line a baking sheet with parchment paper.
2. In a bowl combine the cream cheese and yogurt. Blend until creamy.
3. Add in the cocoa powder, vanilla extract, honey if using and coffee. Mix until well blended.
4. Using a small scoop, take tablespoon sized dollops of the mixture and place on the baking sheet.

5. Top each with a chocolate covered espresso bean, if desired.
6. Place in the freezer and freeze for at least 4 hours or overnight for best results.

Sweet and Salty Margarita Frozen Yogurt Squares

The combination of salt, lime zest and mint make this a perfect dessert for when you are craving something refreshing, but not too sweet.

Serves: 6-9

Ingredients

3 cup plain Greek yogurt

1 3 ounce package sugar free lime flavored gelatin

1 cup boiling water

½ cup fresh lime juice

1 tablespoon lime zest

1 teaspoon coarse salt

1 tablespoon fresh mint, finely chopped.

Directions

1. Line a 9"x9" baking dish with parchment paper
2. Prepare the gelatin by adding the boiling water to the gelatin powder and stirring to dissolve. Set aside to let cool slightly.
3. Add the Greek yogurt and lime juice to the bowl and mix on medium speed until creamy and fluffy.
4. In a food processor, combine the lime zest, salt, and fresh mint. Pulse until finely ground.

5. Add to the creamy gelatin mixture, and stir well.

6. Pour the mixture into the baking pan and place in the freezer.

7. Freeze for at least 4 hours, or overnight for best results.

8. Cut into 9 squares before serving.

Strawberry Rhubarb Ice Cream Sauce

Eating sugar free doesn't mean that you have to skip ice cream sauce, or settle for bland options from your grocer's shelf. Tart and sweet fruit is combined with orange juice as a substitute for sugar in this recipe. This sauce is just as delicious on pancakes and other desserts as it is on ice cream.

Serves: 6

Ingredients

2 cups fresh strawberries, quartered

1 cup fresh rhubarb, cut into small pieces

½ cup orange juice (no additional sugar added)

1 tablespoon cornstarch

2 tablespoons water

1 teaspoon ground ginger

2 teaspoons honey (optional)

Directions

1. Combine the strawberries, rhubarb, and orange juice in a saucepan. Cook over medium heat until boiling.
2. In a small bowl combine the cornstarch and water. Whisk until smooth.

3. Add the cornstarch, ginger, and honey, if using, to the sauce pan.
4. Stir and continue to cook for 5-7 minutes, or until sauce thickens, over medium heat.
5. Remove from heat and let cool. Sauce will be fairly chunky. If a smoother consistency is desired, place in a blender and blend until desired smoothness in attained.
6. Place sauce in an airtight container and store in the refrigerator until ready to use.

CONCLUSION

I hope that you have enjoyed this journey through sugar free frozen summer treats. The beautiful flavors of the season offer endless possibilities for satisfying your sweet tooth while still maintaining your healthy lifestyle. You now have many options for creating and enjoying delicious summer desserts that you can enjoy during a quiet summer sunset, or during festive family gatherings. Don't feel confined to the exact recipes included in this book. Feel free to experiment and switch out fruits and flavors. The only limit to the possibilities is what is available at your local farmers market. Enjoy and have a happy, safe summer.

ABOUT THE AUTHOR

Sarah Spencer, who lives in Canada with her husband and two children, describes herself as an avid foodie who prefers watching the Food Network over a hockey game or NCIS! She is a passionate cook who dedicates all her time between creating new recipes, writing cookbooks, and her family, though not necessarily in that order!

Sarah has had two major influences in her life regarding cooking, her Grandmother and Mama Li.

She was introduced to cooking at an early age by her Grandmother who thought cooking for your loved ones was the single most important thing in life. Not only that, but she was the World's Best Cook in the eyes of all those lucky enough to taste her well-kept secret recipes. Over the years, she conveyed her knowledge and appreciation of food to Sarah.

Sarah moved to Philadelphia when her father was transferred there when Sarah was a young teenager. She became close friends with a girl named Jade, whose parents owned a Chinese take-out restaurant. This is when Sarah met her second biggest influence,

Mama Li. Mama Li was Jade's mother and a professional cook in her own restaurant. Sarah would spend many hours in the restaurant as a helper to Mama Li. Her first job was in the restaurant. Mama Li showed Sarah all about cooking Asian food, knife handling, and mixing just the right amount of spices. Sarah became an excellent Asian cook, especially in Chinese and Thai food.

Along the way, Sarah developed her own style in the kitchen. She loves to try new flavors and mix up ingredients in new and innovative ways. She is also very sensitive to her son's allergy to gluten and has been cooking gluten-free and paleo recipes for quite some time.

More Books from Sarah Spencer

Shown below are some of her other books. To check any of them out, just click on the book cover you like. Follow Sarah and join in her great love of cooking!

Made in the USA
San Bernardino, CA
08 March 2018